Fame
&
Glory

Love, Sanity, Christ, and Poetry

Published by, Clea McLemore

ISBN: 978-0-9961442-0-9 (paperback)
ISBN: 978-0-9961442-1-X (eBook)

Library of Congress Control Number: 2015918437

Fame & Glory: Love, Sanity, Christ, and Poetry
Poetry Collection
Published in 2015 by Clea McLemore

Edited by, E.M. McLemore
Cover Photograph Courtesy of, Brittany Howard
Cover Design Clea McLemore, Dare2CareComputers, LLC

Inquiries & special discounts for bulk purchases can be made by contacting the publisher and author at: books@CleaMcLemore.com

Visit the author online at:
www.CleaMcLemore.com
Facebook.com/CleaMcLemore
Twitter.com/theClMac
Instagram.com/theClMac

First Edition

Contents

PART 1 – ALL FOR LOVE   1

I WANT TO READ YOU A POEM (AGE 31)   2

SCARED   4

IF YOU FORGET ME TOO   5

DAYDREAM   9

FOR YOU, MOTHER   12

KNOCK, KNOCK   15

MY FREEDOM IS GONE (AGE 15)   19

SEPTEMBER   20

ACCEPTANCE (AGE 20)   22

CHEERS TO YOU   24

UNSTUCK   27

THIS IS SUCH A LOVE POEM   30

I WISH: A LETTER TO MY CHILD (AGE 31)   32

PART 2 – ALL FOR SANITY   35

OPTIONS (AGE 19)   36

SELFISH   38

NO MORE   38

FAME AND GLORY [LITTLE BLACK GIRL] (AGE 24)   39

A KISS   41

LESSON LEARNED [A SQUIRREL'S LIFE]   41

TO BE WITH SHE, OR TO BE WITH ME? (AGE 20)   42

PIECES   47

FEELINGS (AGE 20)   48

CHECKMATE   51

INDECENCY   52

THE ROBBER   55

WRINKLES   57

SHOOTING STAR (AGE 25)   58

THE LAST TIME   59

PART 3 – ALL FOR CHRIST   62

DEAR WORLD (AGE 27)   63

THE BEST OF ME   66

DIRECTION   67

JESUS TAKE THE WHEEL (AGE 27)   68

ALL MY DAY (AGE 27)   69

ALL OVER THE PLACE   71

PLASTIC   72

YOU ARE THE MORE   73

WALK   78

CLOSE   81

A COUPLE, AFTER GOD'S OWN HEART   83

THIS TOO   88

PART 4 – ALL FOR POETRY   90

THRIFT STORE   91

HAIKU - 1, 2, 3   91

WRITER'S BLOCK   92

MR. PEN & MRS. INK   94

ONE TEAR   96

WATER   100

THE DEPTHS OF POETRY   101

AUCTION   103

DARE   103

SLEEP   104

UN-LOVING YOU   106

THE STAGE (AGE 26)   110

Clea | Κλέος (Greek) | translated **Kleos**:

- To Praise, Acclaim, Fame
- Her Father's Renown, Glory of the Father
- That which is heard or spoken, to call

Forward:

Joy for writing was discovered in Junior High school, after reading a poem written by a friend. The youthful prose captivated already sensitive senses, and I was lured into its promising endless sea of freedom. After the pangs of losing a notebook of poetry in 8th grade, my writing ceased. And I only gazed in awe, at the flow of Robert Frost, and the sweet gentleness of Longfellow during Literature class.

However; poetry was reintroduced personally at the age of 15 after having my first daughter. The only coping mechanism found was to release the disappointment, the shame, and yet the utter blissfulness of it all by writing a poem called "My Freedom is Gone" which was included in Vicksburg High school's annual literature book entitled *Vicksburg Voices*. Releasing that poem relieved the intensity of pressure and the shock of teenage motherhood tremendously and writing has continued to be a close acquaintance even now.

The birth of my second daughter by the age of almost 17, GED, college, love, struggle, family, Christ, an IT career have been fuel upon which to write things. Although vulnerability is expected as a writer, it's a small price to pay for encouraging other young mothers, fathers, parents, and just plain common folk that we only come this way once. We must strive to be nothing less than what God has destined us to be. No matter the obstacle, no matter the sin. When failure is not an option, success is the outcome.

My belief is that every person has a poem. Perhaps you have yet to read it, or the younger poet is hard at work crafting his jewels. Maybe it's being created in a young child or spouse; to one day write one of their own, but there is a poem in all. My hope is that this book will lead you to that poem or in some way quench that inherent thirst all have, as you find the one to call your own.

It is with great pleasure that I present to you a semi-autobiographical book of poetry that displays a Southern girl, who climbs beyond the voices and piercing eyes of society's statistical notations of her future. One who tells stories seen through the eyes of others, who discovers the difference between healthy and unhealthy relationships, rediscovers her rightful place in Christ, and continues to accept nothing less than embracing her destiny. The journey of pursuing dreams hidden underneath valleys, and ocean tides of life are filled with infinite smiles, burdens, joys, and trials. This book entails some of the hidden most parts of me, as I pursue the journey to God's *Fame and Glory*.

Clea McLemore

Because of Eva, Eric, Ash, & Ni for being my inspiration…family & friends for being a rock: to all of those who ever believed I could

…& to JC (Jesus Christ), the One who makes *all things possible and creates all things new.*

ON THE PAGES OF MY LIFE, YOU HAVE REVEALED YOUR GLORY.

Fred Hammond

PART 1

All for Love

I Want to Read You a Poem (age, 30)

I want to
sit on a Mississippi porch swing in spring
read you poetry again.

let you lie upon a welcoming lap
while I stroke your head
allow your heart to be comforted

as poets devotedly describe blessed weather
while we fall in love
with their melodies together.

I want to read you a poem
so, delicate and tender
that gently coerces you to remember
full moons, whispering trees
autumn wings that spread whispering leaves
and leave you?
I never.

I aim to spend both lifetimes together
as we raise a family now
worship in eternity
then,
fall in love with a better love
all over again.

I want to
bend knees with you and pray

that the love we found will stay
in God's most blessed will
until destiny
is fulfilled.

© summer 2014

Scared

You wonder,

Why

I don't love you

Well,

I didn't know my heart was so afraid until

I felt it feeling

Familiar feelings.

Truth is I'm scared,

That your love is not perfect enough

To

Cast out all fears[1]

I suspect

It puffs up the eyes and shortens the years.

---

[1] I John 4:18 King James Version. There is no fear in love; but perfect love casteth out fear: because fear hath torment. He that feareth is not made perfect in love.

If you Forget Me Too[2]

Let me tell you this:

I know,

if I smell

the honeysuckle on the green bush

tapping at my door.

The cool vine, emerald and sun kissed lush

dripping, with the cold dew of morning

sweetly scented;

If I walk

toward the fearless storm,

the perceptible precipitation

leaking on the roofs of houses,

my will drives me to you.

It's like

my resolve, my resentments,

were schools of fish

that swim

---

[2] This piece, is in response to Pablo Neruda's "If You Forget Me." Neruda, Pablo. "If You Forget Me" *Earth-Shattering Poems*. Ed. Liz Rosenberg, New York, NY: Henry Holt and Company, LLC, 1998. 45-46. Print.

toward the bait on your hook.

Well now,

If for some reason you lose interest in me

I shall have a reason to lose interest in you.

If you awake one morning,

and don't know my name

don't try to remember it,

because I will not know your name either.

If you spend days and nights,

climbing staffs

crescendoing

along treble clefs

Streaming my heart like bows do violins,

with musical melody of notes

(only you can play in forte

that, move my soul)

and you decide

to throw me back into the loveless sea

I will haunt you.

Like trails of snail slime

oozing down sidewalks of life in time.

[If you choose

to let me slip away

from the places I know best,

bear in mind

at that second,

I shall have to be the fat lady that sings and says,

"It's over!"]

But

if like a flash of lightning,

Piercing through darkness like platinum knives

you make your presence known

Like the smell of bacon frying early morn,

as the sunlight tickles your eyes

Before they rise;

You give in and surrender to the growling

in your stomach

only I can feed

In me,

those dams of raging waters are released

nothing is drowned nothing evaporated

all is kept, saturated

inside the sponge of my heart.

As long as your feelings

are constant and unwavering

like my old Grandfather's clock and chain

I'll be the remedy

that keeps you sane.

Daydream

I've lived my whole life without you
So the day you left, I didn't forget how to keep on living
the Sun, didn't forget how to rise in the east
how to set in the west

The birds didn't forget how to sing,
the clouds didn't forget how to float, on air
the wind didn't forget how to blow in and
rinse your scent away

And I,
didn't forget to remember you
today.

I've lived my whole life without you,
up until now, no memories of you were to be found;
You were simply the cause, of a smile,
throughout the day, in a daydream
So when you appeared in the flesh you were everything loved
seemed
to be
to me.

But as time passed, and
I began to pull back the layers of your love
the true colors of lust began to shine through
And I knew
in my heart
that,
destiny was not in the corner that
pushed in favor of our forever
it lied upon the lines of
temporarily
and devastation
would be an understatement
of what came over me

Because, in you
[I thought] I found
keys-
that unlocked the hidden closets of love
holding secrets to mysteries that hearts die of

The whole world was mine,
for a moment;
but it slipped out of clutching hands--in an instant!
When I glanced, I saw the smoke from its fire,

dying

in the distance.

So, as I fail to forget and

subconsciously remember to remember you

I ask myself,

"If I missed it?"

And even though I know better,

There are moments-

you become

the cause

of a smile

throughout the day

in a daydream.

© February 2011

For You, Mother

I wanted to write a poem for you,

But couldn't find the words to say.

So, shall I compare thee to a Summer's Day? [3]

Of course, thou art more lovely

Indeed, more temperate than they.

Because the light of your love shines forever

And summer days, they fade away

But at their peak, they attempt to meet

The goodness found in you.

But you shine brighter any day

In everything you do

And it is you,

Whatever a day will always bring

Whatever a sun will always sing, is you [4]

---

[3] Shakespeare, William. "Shall I Compare thee to a Summer's Day?" The Random House Treasury of Favorite Love Poems. Ed. Random House, Inc. New York, NY: Random House, Inc., 2002. 50. Print.

[4] Cummings, E.E. "[I carry your heart with me (I carry it in]" Poetry Foundation. Poetry Foundation, n.d. Web. 29 October 2015.

You've clothed yourself with strength and honor

And you wear them well

That's why Virtuous[5] is the word your children use

to describe you when they tell

The world of their most prized possession;

A mirror, of Love's reflection.

Before the foundation of the world did He call you;

With His hands, placed you above my hopes and dreams

Knowing you'd see me as He does,

Looking past my faults and trivial things,

Seeing me for who I am,

Not how I'm seen

Oh the wisdom, knowledge, and joy you bring,

You house the melodies that make my heart sing.

So on this day, at this hour,

Honor is given to whom honor is due[6]

This is just a whisper dear mother, of

---

[5] *Proverbs 31:10 Who can find a virtuous woman? for her price is far above rubies.*

[6] *Romans 13:7 Render therefore to all their dues: tribute to whom tribute is due; custom to whom custom; fear to whom fear; honour to whom honour.*

how much I love you.

Knock, Knock

I let you in.

Opened the doors to my world

Wide as the widest tide in the deepest ocean

The one that collides with continents,

Moves sail boats and cruise liners,

Carries fish of sea from lake to river

That same tide, carried you to me.

So when you knocked on the steel doors that were bolted shut-

I began by removing the chain,

Turning the dead-bolt to open,

Using the one key I had left

Hope-

And I let you in.

Just as you were

Broke, bruised, and damaged goods,

But you were no good for me.

Your work ethic, was no good

Your commitment, no good,

Your word, no good

And, for some reason then, I never understood
Why I couldn't love the wrong out of you
In order to make you right.
I saw you, for your potential
For the man I knew you could be
Never for the man you are, or were
The man you would be, if you weren't
With me.

I simply
Ignored all warnings
Flashing lights, invisible actions,
Dead End signs that lead
To ended roads…

We should have parted there

But like cheese to rats
We both kept coming back to retrieve scraps
That failed to suffice, leftovers, only enough to maintain
a little longer.
Towards the end of our relationship
We both knew a little longer had grown up
Into a little less,

Our time was counter-clockwise

hours became seconds

The goodbyes were in mass production

It wasn't long before,

I saw you at the crossroads.

I let you in.

Opened the doors to my universe

Wide as the sky is to the human eye

 And you changed my world

Turned it upside down,

Caused unstable houses to fall

You brought in black clouds, hurricanes

High winds, heavy rains

Flooded naiveties, doubts, insecurities

These things you shook up and more

Until only the best was left of me. Kept the good

The bad, the 'ugly' with you left the rest of me.

Now, my dignity, my self-worth

Will not be compromised.

And those bolts will stay locked

Until you realize

You'll have to bring more to the table

than

the physical wedding bed

Before I let you in.

My Freedom is Gone (age 15)

My freedom is gone because a child is here,

Every passing day brings to me another tear,

Why, Oh why, did this happen to me?

Is this a dream or

Is this the way things really turned out to be?

My life seems so different and so wrong,

My freedom seems forever gone.

Why didn't I cherish it when it was here?

Now that it's gone things seem so unclear.

But misery is not all that my child has brought,

By me teaching her I am constantly being taught,

About the joys motherhood can bring,

In my life there could be no greater thing.

My freedom IS gone, but more love is here,

Now my future seems forever clear.

September

The sky is still,
The wind bends down to brush my ear
In early,
September.

Snapshots of seasons taking turns in the spotlight
During their most vulnerable times
Opposing forces
Intertwined-
Not really.

Just yesterday
Summer lay
Out beneath its glory, fully bloomed
And we picked its petals,
Way too soon.

Only lonely leaves pass through the winds
of this gentle night;
No colors, of summer will survive our fall.

Seemingly still stars spread out across

A seemingly still black backdrop

Appearances do often deceive,

Despite-

Waging wars,

To believe.

© fall 2012

Acceptance (age 20)

Don't refuse me.

Don't say no to the love I offer you

Don't speak before you think

Yes, think first-

Think about the love felt in the air

when we were both trapped in

our unending maze of it.

The disease and gift of being truly in love

Remember when...

Remember when I held you in my arms,

Remember when words weren't a necessary means for

communication between us

Mere thoughts, a simple smile.

Remember when that was enough,

Remember when that was all that was needed to say;

I love you.

While keeping these things in mind

Don't push away my hand when I now offer it to you

Don't look at me like I'm a different person

Like you don't know me.

Look further inside,

Find the person that you once loved,

Find the reason why that love was lost

Find this out at any cost

Because, that love can't be bought again

That love is not redeemable at any store

Can't be exchanged or traded for anything more,

Can't be purchased or mimicked by any fake me.

That love was made between us,

That love can only be shared with

the two persons that made it

you and me,

Remember when...

And while keeping these things in mind,

Remember those memories can still reinvent themselves

and become a reality

If you just let them be

Remember when

Remember us

Remember you

Then remember me.

Cheers to You

I loved you so hard
I'm talking sweat
Tears, tissue of muscle
Climbed over hills
Reached the peak of mountain-topped fears
And still pursued,
The incredible journey of loving you.

I loved you so tender
I'm talking hands marinated
In patient's sweet savor of
Faith, hope, and longing lands
My future was planned
To carefully embrace your hidden most places
For as long as love allowed

Shoved pride to side
Humbled myself to love you in spite of,
not foreseeing
I'd love you too long.

I loved you so long.

I'm talking
Long after
Love soared
Then subsided

When it no longer abided safely tucked away beneath
Dank corridors of common's truthful sense.
When the Sun found our, rabbit hole
Its light exposed frail bones and famished souls
Yet, I loved you long after hunger pangs

Unaware as
Body shut down
Went into hibernation
To survive the long cold winter
Of a growling soul's starvation

I loved you so
I'm talking memories that cannot lie,
That fade some, but do not die
I'm talking gratitude, even from the pain
Let's toast, cheers to you and to the fact;
I do not love *him* the same
Because of you

Now I can
love him
Better.

Unstuck

Stuck in the middle of this rhyme and reason,

My mind's telling me to slow down but my heart says

It's not leaving, in fact it's cleaving;

Even though you cause it pain and keep it bleeding.

It keeps right on believing, that

Love will make a way.

Even though it made a wrong turn yesterday, and

Came to a dead end today

One expects, hope can and should apply in these particular

situations as well, but

with young love;

One can never really tell

What portion of the heart needs the most feeding

Which words were spoken from the soul-

Without intentions of deceiving,

Or, which lies to dismiss and

Which ones to keep on believing.

I attempt to follow my heart but

It keeps on misleading…the way.[7]

I could re-count the days but time doesn't permit

and, I refuse to sit around

and wait on

Later maybe, never, and possible forevers

You've always told me I was clever;

So don't expect any less of me now

Expect more, above and beyond

Especially since I can see clearly now,

The rain is gone,

The pain is gone,

The blame is gone

Almost lost portions of my character while

dazed in your song

Yet, if I could count the ways I loved you

They'd be like the days that are long,

The wicked things that are wrong,

You and your first love's first song…

See, I loved hard

---

[7] Jeremiah 17:9 The heart is deceitful above all things, and desperately wicked: who can know it?

I loved long.

I tried to love you, until

All the pain was gone,

And still, love you just because.

With no intentions of letting go

Until you desired to be let go

So, don't blame me

Blame yourself

You are the reason that I left.

This is Such a Love Poem

As I wait for him; I know that he exists

Because he appears to me in daydreams like epiphanies

He sends Morse code messages by wind and ear;

To gently whisper, "I am near."

Somewhere out there

My love is calling

I feel his breaths as I breathe mine

As I lay down to rest, his head too inclines.

My Love,

I have never seen you with a pair of eyes, never

Obliged my fingertips to brush your blackberry skin

But that doesn't make you any less tangible.

To believe in someone you cannot see

To trust in something you can only feel

Doesn't make you any less, real

So in the meantime,

While you're waiting to find

The me, that makes you whole;

Be patient my Dear

Dissolve thoughts of doubt and fear

Because in due time,

I'll be so close to you that

God will consider us one flesh.

And I know you've had good and better before, but

I assure you

This One is the best.

Together, we'll make this place a whole new world

While others chase their dreams,

We'll simply walk beside ours; Palm-to-palm,

Finger locked-to-knuckle, Hope-to-love

Striding along the sands of today

Riding the waves of tomorrow.

We'll make sandcastles of our sorrows

And watch them wash away and

submerge into the sea of forgetfulness.

Guide me, into your wilderness

So I may wonder wildly in your love

While we

Fall, in love.

© summer 2010

I Wish: A Letter to My Child (age 31)

My child,

I wish I could protect you

From sunburns of reality,

Life's fragilities are likely

To scorch your delicate skin.

I desire to protect you from awaking early mornings

Facing shattered mirrors from opposition

Where friction burns dreams-

While the world idolizes materialistic things.

Years have the tendency to suffocate asthmatic hopes

I'd never want you to choke

on the truth, it must be swallowed.

No matter how large, sharp or unpleasant the taste

I face it too...

      I can't protect you from this.

Protecting would only cripple your immune system

And you must learn to fight those deadly invaders

No, not for survival-

That only gets you through

A single sunrise, another sunset, perhaps one full moon
You my child, must learn to conquer.

Although, I desire to be your shield for always
Mortality lacks the tools of forever
I've done my best to use seconds wisely
Remember, when I taught you how to
Walk on wobbly legs?
Well, they're stronger now, you can run instead.

And now that time has grown tender
I can only prepare meals of knowledge that
Tingle taste buds of determination's momentum
Pour tall glasses of wisdom that propel feet to leap
Over obstacles and arms to soar for life's more.

I live for you, heart burns, soul yearns
And I
Hope throughout the years
I've done enough
To protect you.

© 2014

PART 2

All for Sanity

Options <small>(age 19)</small>

What do I do when my options have fled?
When those series of questions
constantly reenter my head,
When the road suddenly cuts itself off
Without a warning, a sound, or a sign

Like a fallen grape searching for her maker,
the source of life,
the True Vine[8]

Who can I turn to
when my days become as dark as nights
And the empowerment of my inner self
burns until it can burn no more
burns until it ignites.

Into a raging fire with no sign of ending, no sign of ending

yet,
ending only to find a new beginning

---

[8] John 15:5 I am the vine, ye are the branches: He that abideth in me, and I in him, the same bringeth forth much fruit: for without me ye can do nothing.

a new source of power greater than the Sun.

with enough energy to keep me still

so I'll no longer run

No longer run from the fear of pain

No longer run from the shame I've gained

No longer run from the past I've left

No longer run from Clea

run no longer from

self.

When, why, how, what, where? I ask myself

"Does anyone know, does anyone care?"[9]

---

[9] Jeremiah 29:11 For I know the thoughts that I think toward you, saith the LORD, thoughts of peace, and not of evil, to give you an expected end.

Selfish

Gave you the best of me,

Wasn't much left of me;

Still, you then

wanted the rest of me

No More

I've had enough.

My stomach is full,
It lacks the capacity to be filled with any more

Of your, luscious lies.

Fame and Glory [Little Black Girl] (age 24)

Little black girl where are you?

Under a house, under a shoe, under a…who?

Because it seems as if you've vanished into thin air

And reappeared as a thing, not a person, over there.

Little black girl, where are you?

Has someone hurt you along your way?

On the outside you look fine,

full of life, red as wine.

Bling blinging, flossing breasts and

dropping backs

Riding in vans, hoopties, and Cadillac's

Was it the lies that led you to believe?

You'd be the only one to carry his seed

Because you used to sit high with kings and

be referred to as queens

Demand respect and nothing less;

Now you exchange your worth for nothingness.

You shining on the outside,

But there's darkness in your eyes

That tell another story.

Little black girl, when did you fall

so far away,

From glory?

A Kiss

The wind kissed the shy flower petals,

They danced with delight

A kiss

Was all they needed

To make things alright.

Lesson Learned [A Squirrel's Life]

I saw a squirrel

Through the thicket

Of reviving trees

Treading; to the rocky outermost branch

He takes a chance

To find the food he needs.

© 2013

To Be with She, Or to be with Me? (age 20)

To be with she?

Or, to be with me?

That is the question I ask of you when there's talk of we

There can be no in-between linings amongst us

Invisible to my heart you see-

I feel you when she's near you.

I sense her looming presence when

you're here with me

You must choose one between us

Or, I'll make the choice for we

I can no longer fight these battles,

wage these wars

  just to be with you

Settle for less than I know I'm worth

   just to be with you

Compromise my worth,

    just to be with you.

If I did,

I'd be belittling myself
  just to be with you
Our relationship would lack in health
If the truth I withheld from self;
And for you,
I would do anything
but this
I cannot do.

Just so you and I can be a we
I not just an I, you not just a he
But the problem is there's still she,
And that she is not me!

I can no longer run these races for your love
Hope that I win the gold so
You'll think more of
How I can be your everything
All that you need
When deep down I know
your problem is merely
Selfishness and greed

I provide love unconditionally

It never ends,

And the end of my love for you cannot be seen

What happened to you being my King and I your Queen?

Has our kingdom become weak and dismembered?

Can we replay that day we fell in love

back in 99 of September?

Is a flashback needed to make you remember?

Or have you memories become corrupt and

in return misremembered?

But the truth is,

none of these things matter

If mattered they did

my heart wouldn't feel like a woman battered

My dreams wouldn't seem to be lost and shattered

And this poem

would not contain these adjectives of this Subject matter

If only

If

Only

'we'

mattered to you.

Then,

you and I would be a we,

Not just you a he or I just a me,

Unable to see clearly through this difficult relationship,

Maybe the problem is the love we seem to both cherish so

Never depriving ourselves to the pain of letting go

Because…

Since the beginning of this

My lips continuously long for the touch of your lips

To seal this love with a brand new kiss

Because without it

I don't know if I could get through it

[there's no definition for this]

Marian Webster was the closest thing to it

Yes,

you are the personification of my love

And even with that,

one has a hard time grasping the concept of

Our love

But just like Is,

is

Is,

We just are...

But we are no longer together anymore,

Because I've made the choice for we

To leave those bitter, sweet memories behind

and let them be

Merely bitter sweet memories of we

And to become once more of who we were before

I just a me, you just a he.

To be with she,

To be with she,

And not to be with me

And not to be with… me

This is the choice I've made for us both

….the next time there's talk of we

Pieces

I was one whole woman when I met you.

Two eyes, one heart, two arms and two legs

Heart beating freely, wondering, but

Not needing assistance to keep on breathing

You left, but not before dismantling me

Like a picture, pixel by pixel

Like a book, page by page

Like a poem line by line

Until

I

Fell apart because of you.

Feelings (age 20)

These feelings I have inside,
I mean the pain, the anguish, the loneliness, the worry, the fear
Will they ever go away?
Or will years and time replay themselves and
they all will find a way to stay

Please don't stay, Go away

To the highest mountain, to the darkest cave
to that distant star,
to your dark. cold. grave.

Please don't stay, Go away

Let me find my solitude, discover my peace
carve my path stay strong not weak
And to that indescribable feeling that words cannot place
State your mission, plead your case,
Or else get out, you can't stay,
You must go away.

And to that feeling called love, why bother me?

I don't need affection and caressing,
I can stand alone, on my own
Why do I need a man?
To hurt me?
Confuse me?
Verbally abuse me?
Buy me off then think he can use me?

So love,
I'll put you on the back burner
I'll handle my business, and when
The time comes…

Ohhh, I know love and it don't work that way,
It's going to sneak up on me and catch me one day,
But I'm running just as fast as I can, because when love catches
up with me I'll go falling again.

No, no, no, no,
I'm not going to run, not this time
Instead of running away I'm going to look you
straight in your face and deal with you,

See

Deep down inside I want you, but
Don't treat me like that-
Make me smile then cry, make me happy then sad
Please love don't do me so bad

I trusted you once, twice, thrice and
you slapped me in my face
And from that day on I promised myself I was through with you.

But one more time, maybe two
I'll put aside my fears wipe my tears,
Try love, try to love, try to be loved, and
last but not least,
I'll try you?
Love

Checkmate

I'd like to think

We could live our lives

and, put away

the chess we play.

Move pieces

Into houses onto Ash fields under sunrays of better days

And dare to play in April's showers without paranoia

You'll checkmate the king that

guards the castle

of hearts.

©2013

Indecency

It was bad enough you hurt me once,

but countless times;

Was simply inhumane.

To continuously take away bits of my breath

Crumb by crumb,

and say everything will be okay.

To deprive me of the sense of touch, since

I can't feel anymore,

Due to how you touched me.

The sense of sight since, every tangible object my eyes meet now

Become distorted from the memories of past times your lies

greeted then.

See,

You did a great deal more than dogs that stray

You tore at my confidence, page by page

Dismantled my dreams, piece by piece

Until I came apart in you.

Yet it didn't stop there,

You, lied on love, more than hate does

Showed empathy, while thinking of others;
You even cried, fake tears that held real water
And acquired multiple supporters
for counterfeit causes.

And here I am,
Forgiving you again, just as I once did daily
No grudges, for not loving me,
(Life works that out)
Forgive you for not caring
That it was hard enough,
having two children by the age of seventeen,
You didn't care that I had to
feed, clothe, and educate children such as your own;
On my own

Still you,
Continued to smile slyly while holding out eager hands.
You saw me spend many a night,
Battling the odds to receive my degree
And you knew of my dreams as a writer
But consciously
You ruined years of my life;
Out of what you referred to as 'convenience'

See

that's how

So many lives are changed for sake of

The _____

The Robber

I saw a robber once when I was 10

In a rundown gas station.

He was wearing a red bandana

that looked like Swiss cheese.

I could still see where his eyes were supposed to be,

But instead there were two void spaces filled with coal, waiting to

be lit by a fire.

He glanced in my direction.

I closed my eyes hoping he could no longer see me, since

I could no longer see him.

But his odor gave him away.

Invisible stink bombs lurked around him,

like ghosts searching for revenge.

Somewhere along the way the robber had picked up

a rotten friend.

I managed to squeeze underneath one of the shelves with the

Little Debbie© treats

I made myself an addition to their puzzle piece

Even though they yawned and crackled before readjusting

I could hear the clerk now, frantically chanting,

"Take the money, you can have it!"

The robber centered his attention

towards the back door.

I dropped my head to the floor.

He looked around but I couldn't be found

So he snatched the money and ran.

I once saw a robber when I was 10.

My friends thought I should have been frightened

But to me it felt like a Blockbuster hit

And I didn't want to split

the proceeds, indeed

That's how,

I became

The Robber.

Wrinkles

I stand here today
More of a woman, less of a child.

Realizing tears,
Are little puddles that have to be
Stepped over, waded through, and walked in
In order to get
to the place needed

And the wrinkles on my forehead
Are imprints of rocky roads traveled,
Some longer than others
Others harder than some
But necessary
To
Have led me here.

Shooting Star (age 25)

If I was a star,

I'd feel like rockets and laser beams were shooting at me

I'd think the darkness of night

devised plans daily

in an attempt to steal my light.

I'd cry crystal tears

during flight

mourn the loss of innocence

but still shine bright.

Since,

some say stars stay, still I'd feel

like

The odds were against me

But then I'd raise the bar

Just be me-

A shooting star.

The Last Time

Each time we come to an end
it seems like the last time.

Like the time before that and
the time before
neither was the end, but
there's something contrasting about this time.

It will not mimic nor duplicate times before
when you threw away love; showed me the door.
This time there will be no involve crying,
Anguish, newly formed tears,
Nor hurt and pain dished out for years
No, not this time.

You will soon observe this time is unalike the others
I have the strength to say no,
The power to let go
My heart is not impaired
the pain has not deepened
I have not weakened
This time.

I'm free of any doubts,
Don't need man to ease pain;
I have God to sustain

Now,
the last time I was a, little naïve
the time before, easily deceived
but not this time.

This time I'm more seasoned, a little wiser,
and you my dear are no longer the desire

No goodbye kiss, no lover's bliss;
Use the time before when you thought that was it
call that the last time.

My heart is out of cheeks to turn
It's also in agreement
That we've past
Our last time.

PART 3

All for Christ

Dear World (age 27)

(from the Lord, to me)

You thought you were one step ahead;

You were smart, but not wiser than I.

You were one step from the grave,

You were ready to die

I tried to save you with My love,

Even though you replied

"Don't save me, My Love, I am ready to die" [10]

But your soul wasn't Heaven bound,

And I couldn't let you go until I knew you'd found

The Wonder,

that makes worlds go round.

It was a journey-

Me, dragging you along,

you, pushing Me away

you, telling Me to leave

Me, asking you to stay

Us both traveling down a long road,

---

[10] Romans 6:23 For the wages of sin is death; but the gift of God is eternal life through Jesus Christ our Lord.

neither of us headed in the same direction

your aim was fool's gold

Mine was divine perfection.

(my Response)

I knew each morning, facing mirrors

Self-Reflection

Will be the only one standing before You Lord

While others will have turns separately

Knowing the world can't save me

From a hell that's not theirs

And my friends can't house me in a Heaven that

We're both unworthy to enter…

I've been running for a while now,

I'm ready to repent

"I am a sinner."

You captured whole heart,

With mercy, grace, Your unwavering love

And as always You've protected me

Never neglected me as I did You;

You've been too true to be a man

You have to be God

Because I was lost, but You found me

I once was blind, now I see[11]

You have revealed Your truth:

that nothing shall ever separate me

from the love of You[12]

Neither death nor life, principalities nor powers,

things present nor things to come;

Shall separate me from the love of You, Lord

in Jesus Christ Your Son[13]

Tomorrow is not promised, so I thank Him for today

For giving an ear to hear, knees that bend, and

A mind to pray.

---

[11] John 9:25 He answered and said, Whether he be a sinner or no, I know not: one thing I know, that, whereas I was blind, now I see.

[12] Romans 8:35 Who shall separate us from the love of Christ? shall tribulation, or distress, or persecution, or famine, or nakedness, or peril, or sword?

[13] Romans 8:38-39 For I am persuaded, that neither death, nor life, nor angels, nor principalities, nor powers, nor things present, nor things to come, Nor height, nor depth, nor any other creature, shall be able to separate us from the love of God, which is in Christ Jesus our Lord.

The Best of Me

If time is everything and

He is Author

Of all we perceive

He never runs late,

Tarrying is not one of His traits

So, I'll align my watch with His

Knowing perfection is His specialty

Let Him sear off the bad,

Create in me a clean heart[14]

And keep the rest of me

---

[14] Psalm 51:10 Create in me a clean heart, O God' and renew a right spirit within me.

Direction

When the world tries to drown me

In its sea of sin

I don't want to just stay afloat or

wade in the water

I want a big boat

That won't sink or sway

And the Compass of Christ to guide my way

Jesus Take the Wheel (age 27)

Need to write, must write, have to right

wrongs in life;

Procrastination, has mass-murdered visionaries for centuries,

There are no guarantees so I

Stay on bowed knees,

And since faith without works is dead[15]

I want mine to live outside my head

Let my works be witness to my faith

And pages of my life, reflections of God's grace.

So, adjustments were made

dropped **Pride** off at the bus stop,

along with his friends

Depression, **Anxiety**, and **Distress**

told **Less**, to "Leave me alone" and

Not Enough; to "Stand in the middle of traffic"

Nothing; was left in the backseat,

Jesus took the wheel

And, I chose to ride

On the passenger's side.

---

[15] James 2:26 For as the body without the spirit is dead, so faith without works is dead also.

All My Day (age 27)

My breaths are ever fleeting, heart ever beating[16]

For another moment of Your grace;

Another chance of mercy,

Another glimpse of hope

to one day see You face to face.

Oh Lord,

How I desire to please You, appease Your displeasure

Quenched by my iniquity

Look at my heart, Oh Lord, my desire is to be holy.

You know my need, please, hear my cry

My hope is in You

In You I live and shall not die[17]

No more mediocre, no more second best

You will be first in my life, my All

everything More and nothing less.

Even in my affliction, I yearn for You

Greatly burn for You, still

---

[16] This piece was inspired after reading Psalms 73:25-26. Whom have I in Heaven but thee? and there is none upon earth that I desire beside thee. My flesh and my heart faileth: but God is the strength of my heart, and my portion for ever.
[17] Psalm 118:17 I shall not die, but live, and declare the works of the Lord.

Standing upon the Rock of Ages,

leaning on Your Word

which I know You'll fulfill.

So,

through celebration and sadness

Sanity and madness

Suffering and gladness

I shall not be moved[18]

Bent, but not broken

Tried, yet highly favored

Strategically created

Destined for greatness.

Therefore; through my current reality

I'll search beyond it, to see Your will

To walk in Your way

To wait upon You Lord

To serve You all my day.

---

[18] Psalm 16:8 I have set the Lord always before me: because He is at my right hand, I shall not be moved.

All Over the Place

I'm broken.

don't know where all the pieces are
if I wanted to put them back again;
so,
I trust them, in the Potter's hand[19]

---

[19] Isaiah 64:8 But now, O Lord, thou art our Father; we are the clay, and thou our Potter; and we all are the work of thy hand.

Plastic

The thief is coming

Roaming. running

Going to and fro

In the earth

Walking up and down in it[20]

To kill, steal, and destroy lives[21]

---Surprise!

While some walk through life as clueless as

Plastic Barbie dolls and perplexed Kens

Go to sleep, wake up

walking in circles all over again.

---

[20] Job 1:7 And the LORD said unto Satan, Whence comest thou? Then Satan answered the LORD, and said, From going to and fro in the earth, and from walking up and down in it.
[21] John 10:10 The thief cometh not, but for to steal, and to kill, and to destroy: I am come that they may have life, and that they might have it more abundantly.

You are the More

To see but don't see,

Let distractions fade in the backdrop;

Hear, but don't hear the discord

Hear only what the Spirit of the Lord has to say

Feel, but don't feel

discomfort, but feel

The revitalization of life more abundantly

The causation of fertilization of your faith

He says,

"You come to Me, My dear and I hear;

It's harvest time." [22]

Have faith,

Until end of time as you know it

Pick it up and throw it,

It is your shield for the terror by night and for

the pestilence that walks in darkness[23]

His Word is a lamp unto my feet and a light unto my path[24]

---

[22] Genesis 8:22 While the earth remaineth, seedtime and harvest, and cold and heat, and summer and winter, and day and night shall not cease.

[23] Psalm 91:5-6 Thou shalt not be afraid for the terror by night; nor for the arrow that flieth by day; Nor for the pestilence that walketh in darkness; nor for the destruction that wasteth at noonday.

[24] Psalm 119:105 Thy Word is a lamp unto my feet, and a light unto my path.

In conjunction, faith is what you walk by[25]

So your muscles don't have to move,

Your legs just need to be willing

And it's in that sacrifice that He will be filling your cup.

Causing it to run all over[26] the place, even

Onto the lives of those so wholly connected unto you;

And in blessing, His measures will exceed

limitations that He's placed on mortal minds

Search high and low but none you'll find

Like Him

To whom then will ye liken Him, Or shall He be equal?[27]

He is the One which Is and Was, and Is to Come[28]

There is no sequel.

He hung stars in black spaces,

creating light in dark places.

He painted blue skies behind summer's sunrise

He created birds that push off invisible air, and soar

---

[25] II Corinthians 5:7 For we walk by faith, not by sight:

[26] Psalm 23:5 Thou prepares a table before me in the presence of mine enemies: thou anointest my head with oil; my cup runneth over.

[27] Isaiah 40:25 To whom then will ye liken me, or shall I be equal? Saieth the Holy One.

[28] Revelation 1:8 I am Alpha and Omega, the beginning and the ending, saith the Lord, which is, and which was, and which is to come, the Almighty.

These things are the less, you are the more.

A fabric, fingertips have never touched

A reality, further from any intangible dream

You, are a certain slant of light[29]

Even the moon looks twice,

Because you "Walk in Beauty Like the Night"[30]

A particularly rare package

An effortless captivation of what God's love towards others

should be

Longsuffering, kind, not seeking your own,

but rejoicing in His truth;

Even the young men shall utterly fall,

but the Tree of Life is your youth;

At times you may feel as if you've given so much

You've got nothing left, no time even, for self;

But our God restores,

He takes back

that which has been lost, stolen, and depleted

---

[29] *Dickinson, Emily. "There's a Certain Slant of Light" Poems by Emily Dickinson. Eds. Mabel Loomis Tood and T. W. Higginson, Boston, MA: Roberts Brothers, Publishers, 1892. 106. Print.*

[30] Byron, George Gordon, Lord. "She Walks in Beauty" *The Random House Treasury of Favorite Love Poems*. Ed. Random House, Inc. New York, NY: Random House, Inc., 2002. 33. Print.

When He gives you more than what the devil has stolen
the nation will know; it will be no secret.
 Because, He knoweth the way that you take:
When He hath tried you, you shall come forth as gold

Because gold,
Stands firm, always within its element
Rising under extreme temperatures that test its virtue
Just to show you as it hardens again,
It is indeed gold
Not to be confused with imitation objects that shine
It's element on the Periodic table is number 79.

So keep, pushing like you're pushing,
Even when the walls don't appear to budge
It's making you stronger; He is with you always;
Just a little while longer before He gathers the wheat
Continue to help feed His sheep
And protect them like the Good soldier you are
And He will give you meat,
To fill that hunger in your belly,
Water, to fill your thirst after His righteousness
Sleep to rest your weary body

And a peace that passeth all understanding[31] ©2011

Psalm 91:14-16, KJV

Because you hath set your love upon Him,

Therefore will He deliver you:

He will set you on high, because

you hath known His name.

And when you call on Him, He will answer:

He will be with you in trouble;

The Lord God will deliver you, and honor you

With long life will He satisfy you,

and show you His salvation.

---

[31] Philippians 4:7 And the peace of God, which passeth all understanding, shall keep your hearts and minds through Christ Jesus.

Walk

Lord,
Help me learn how to
get on these two feet and
walk with You[32]

I drag behind at times, fall by the wayside even,
But I don't want You to have to
carry me all along the way
Teach me how to stay
so I can walk.

See, I'm a big girl now,
living in a big world
with what appears to be big problems
and, I know You're the only One
with wisdom and power to solve them.

And I want to
do my part as Your trusted Ambassador for Christ
but in order to fight; I can't be crawling all my life;

---

[32] Genesis 5:24 And Enoch walked with God: and he was not; for God took him.

I know, it's time to give up the bottle

You want to feed me with the meat of Your Word

Lord, teach me how to serve

Teach me how to stand,

Make nerves send signals through my brain that

Tell feet how to move so I can

Walk with You.

Because after walking comes talking

And there are things that need to be said,

ears that need to hear,

hearts that long to fear…nothing.

And it's only Your perfect love that casteth out all fear,

please bring courage near, so I can walk

Boldly in Your ways.

You know the days

Are moving faster than they appear

Jesus is gathering His army,

His time is drawing near[33]

---

[33] Luke 21:8 And he said, Take heed that ye be not deceived: for many shall come in my name, saying, I am Christ; and the time draweth near: go ye not therefore after them.

We must make haste!

You see, time is of the essence,

To get in His face, stay in His presence

Lord,

We implore Your divine assistance!

The flesh is weak, but our spirits are persistent[34]

We won't take no for an answer

we won't let You leave until You bless us

Until You teach us, how

to Walk.

---

[34] Matthew 26:41 Watch and pray, that ye enter not into temptation: the spirit indeed is willing, but the flesh is weak.

Close

Be not far from me oh my Lord,

God of Israel

For I am poured out like clouds drop the water

When You say it's time for their release

So I speak for Peace,

to be still.

My heart is melted like wax

Use this time to mold me again,

from the dust of nothing to the glory of You.

Take Your hands and smooth out the lumps that

block the path to righteousness

turn up the furnace of forgiveness

and purge my sins away,

For I am broken like glass

my skin has been cut deep from the sins that I've sowed;

Wash me, white as snow.

So I may heal, and

fulfill

inwardly.

My vanity is worthless

And all that I'm worth is nothing to mortal man
Because my soul is not for sale;
I was bought with a price a long time ago
Saved from the furnace of hell.

Even when sorrow burns,
In the area where my heart lies
My faith lives and shall not die.
Although, I give up on me
It's only so I can give it all to You
Your will is the wish I hope to consume.

Oh, Be not far from me!
Be closer than close, abide in me
Your secrets, let them hide in me
I'll keep them safe, like my salvation
And declare Your glory throughout this nation.

Renew my mind, so my thoughts are no more
So the only room left, are Yours
So the only room left, are Yours
Selah.

© July 2011

A Couple, After God's Own Heart

For Her

Love makes room

In rooms mostly that are already filled

To capacity,

You've enlarged your room.

To embrace the souls

Of those, who are lost

Even of us that have been found.

Oh flower,

Tell me what it's like

To smell so sweet

Better with time, Mellow as wine

You've blossomed in spite of

Silent whispers and concrete sidewalks

That have strained to block your bloom

Yet, like a tree that stands

You've assumed your position;

Transitioned the surrounding stimuli

Causing stones to crack and crumble

Standing tall while remaining humble.

Allowed God's reigns,

To turn you according to His will

[Chose the road less taken]

Though rain, sleet, and snow

May have temporarily damaged branches

Fall may have blown some of your leaves,

Even then

The beauty of autumn's

Colors shine through,

Just like you do.

For Him

Son, of a Father who's proud

He says push and I will move

Command and I will do

Decree and I will be,

For everyone that asketh receiveth;

And he that seeketh findeth[35]

---

[35] Matthew 7:7-8 Ask, and it shall be given you; seek, and ye shall find; knock, and it shall be opened unto you: For every one that asketh receiveth; and he that seeketh findeth; and to him that knocketh it shall be opened.

And to him that knocketh it shall be opened.

Oh, man of God,

Continue to ask and open your arms wide

Seek and behold, treasures untold

Knock & watch doors unfold

Oh, what joy it is to have a shepherd

For sheep wonder & stray

Lose their way,

While wolves await

With lies on hooks as bait.

Protector,

You lead us back to the fold with love

Do not be afraid-

Only be strong and of a good courage

Fear not,

For the Lord thy God,

He it is that doth go with thee[36]

Has He ever left you?

---

[36] Deuteronomy 31:8 And the Lord, He it is that doth go before thee: He will be with thee, He will not fail thee, neither forsake thee: fear not, neither be dismayed.

Has He ever forsaken you?

Let every man be a liar and

Let our God be true[37]

I'll never leave you

Never forsake you

To Them

Two better halves,

To make one better whole

Years pass, lives unfold

Hearts that together mend

The delicate threads of our Spiritual lives

Wills that bend

To God's own heart

With a life set aside, [for Him]

Oh, to serve God, this is a good thing

To serve in unison as one, is a truth.

Truly He has blessed this union

So, He breathes on you...

---

[37] Romans 3:4 God forbid: yea, let God be true, but every man a liar; as it is written, That thou mightiest be justified in thy sayings, and mightiest overcome when thou are judged.

The harvest is plenty, the laborers are few[38]

But do not fret

You'll stride along the sands of today

While riding the waves of tomorrow,

He'll make sandcastles of your sorrows,

Watch them submerge into the sea of forgetfulness

Leave them there in the wilderness

As you conquer the Promise land.

Two as one

Heart to heart

Hand in hand.

---

[38] Matthew 9:37 Then saith He unto His disciples, "The harvest truly is plenteous, but the labourers are few;

This Too

I'm trying to grab myself
Before, I lose myself.

Self needs help;
No matter the blocks hit, or corners I turn
There's nowhere for Self
To run.

No matter which ear
I cry to
for dear
Life;
The misfortune of my circumstances
seem unfortunate in their eyes.
While, devastation fills mine;
Heavy tears fall down curves on face
Although they are pushed back by previous pains
They fall back again, anyway

Onto the cottony bare white shirt
Onto a naked leg
Sometimes they fall on soft lonely pillows

That lie,

in vacant beds

Excess tragedies

Depress the mind.

Unforeseen catastrophes

With no planned solutions;

I'd rather stay home from the war

And not fight revolutions

All my day.

So lately, yeah it's been rough;

All terrain bicycle riding,

Four wheel driving,

Ford truck

Tough.

And I've been built to last

Because I know in my heart

This too shall pass[39]

---

[39] 'This too shall pass' is often misquoted as being in the Holy Bible but is not. It is thought to reflect, II Corinthians 4:17 For our light affliction, which is but for a moment, worketh for us a far more exceeding and eternal weight of glory;

PART 4

All for Poetry

Thrift Store

You threw me out like old clothes

but became uneasy

when you saw someone else

wearing me.

Haiku - 1, 2, 3

i have to make time

count the ways I love you, there're

not enough days, yet

Writer's Block

A lump lies along the lines of this verse

Though, dormant furies and silent fears

Press,

and *lean* through pens

In an attempt to reach the truthful ink.

I'd much rather write than think

but my writing has experienced blockage

No songs sing here

my mind roams within its carefully crafted cage

like a firefly stuck in a bottle

with no holes,

breathing would be nice,

and since I can't write; right now

I'm having issues with my lungs

This constant inhalation of worldly lusts

Lying, cheating, lusting are cancerous

Can't possibly be healthy,

Tired of holding in frustration,

All out of cheeks to turn[40]

So, I stretch out the palm of my hand

Start striking my pen

In an attempt to beat it…

Into submission.

---

[40] Matthew 5:39 But I say unto you, That ye resist not evil: but whosoever shall smite thee on thy right **cheek**, turn to him the other also.

Mr. Pen & Mrs. Ink

Fight or Flight
I will, I won't, I may, I might
Fight for my life
Or roll like hay
Allow cards to fall where they may.

I've been fighting for so long
Needed to catch a breath
But during the pause had nothing left
No fight to give,
Just a life to live.

Ambitions slept on
Dreams pushed under
Determination's tear stained pillows
Hopes commingled in untidy beds
Motivation hidden in cluttered rooms;
don't want to give up this soon
Too many years left-

So I ask myself,
Will you allow the waves of this world;

Take you where they may?

Or stroke arms and move thighs

through water's lows and highs

To assume position

Swim or sink

Play dumb or think

So,

Made an appointment with my shrinks

Mr. Pen and Mrs. Ink.

© May 17, 2014

One Tear

We're sitting directly across from one another,
A weak legged, faded brown table
stands between us,
barely.

A cool breeze floats through a crack
in the window to join;
The night that marks our final dialogue.

Minutes mingle like houseguests
As we play the childish game of hot potato
Playfully holding on to each other's words
just long enough not to burn
weak bridges that may still lay intact.

Careful and delicate terms
fill empty spaces that
deeply dwell in a place where hearts
secretly
allow them to reside.

Dormant, in-between thoughts

hidden behind reason,
camouflaged in rhyme.

My mind plays run-throughs of prospective conversations that go
somewhat like-

"But, I forgot to tell you...
However;
still I carry you in my heart,
Although...
Never could trust you."

Risks include tangible and intangible assets
that remain crucial factors
In maintaining the quality of life
I wish to exercise,
And no quality of sexual satisfaction can compensate for
Quality of life.

Enough backstabbers and liars crowd the narrow path
that leads to

The road not taken[41]

It should be obvious why

I'd rather not play with fire or

mingle with the enemy.

You initialized and I mutually agreed that separation was in the

best interest of

both parties,

Even more so for me.

And as you gazed into still brown eyes

for the last time,

piercing me with longing looks

I searched all words in my vocabulary,

but Goodbye-

was the one that refused to escape

the confinement of lips

Instead,

all words formed together to make

a single crystal ball

---

[41] Frost, Robert "The Road Not Taken" Poetry Foundation, Poetry Foundation, n.d.
Web. 25 November 2015.

One that enveloped the profound ties

our younger selves shared,

that paved new paths for our journey on-

on our own

One single tear

Filled the corner of my right eye.

I held my breath.

I willed the water not to fall

But fall it did, like waterfalls

into lakes,

into rivers,

into oceans

That

washed our love away.

Water

I pour my heart out on this paper
I pour
Looking behind me before
I leave
Knowing I left parts of it there
Within ink, lying on lines

Because some of these memories
Hurt just too much to leave
Them in my head.

So,
I lay them to rest
Under tidy covers to rest
Try my best to let them lie
Slumber they do but do not die.
They're awaken by ink
that thinks-
with listening paper
and ready pens.

The Depths of Poetry

Loneliness accompanies me on nights like tonight
And I imagine what true love feels like.
Ears that listen, hands that hold
A heart that doesn't judge
Rarely hollow never cold.

Fingertips that wipe
Windshields of tears
From wetness of years.

Love reciprocated
To a complex poet
That doesn't mean to be
But is
Complex.
Simple has long been a desire
But rarely a reality
For a creative mind
I find
It hard to connect
The dots of shallow people
So sometimes I revert, and leap

Into

the depths of poetry.

Auction

Someone

Found

Me.

After being thrown away

Put me on the auction block

But-

No one could

Afford me.

Dare

I dare you to dream;

Close eyelids that cover up eyes

Sleep nightmares of the world away

And wake up on the moon

You shouldn't give up

On

Deferred dreams

So soon.

Sleep

Love is short, but forgetting is so long[42]

Years have passed and I haven't forgotten you

Still, forgetting you

Still, missing you.

I wish our love would have last as long as the grief has

Shipwrecked, and the waters aren't

High enough

To take us away

So, we're stuck in the middle of a wave.

I find a dull knife to splice the ice that's gotten us frozen in

     Time

But part of me wants to stay here

In the only place we have left together,

 Because even in my dreams there's no forever

The cold-

     awakes me

---

[42] *Neruda, Pablo. "Tonight I Can Write" Twenty Love Poems and a Song of Despair. Trans. W. S. Merwin. New York, NY: the Penguin Group, 1976. 77. Print.*

The fire we used to have

                                      forsakes

me.

I shake, I shiver, I quake.
I open my eyes
Now I'm ...
Awake.

©Fall 2010

Un-loving You

I don't know how to un-love you
If it was only as easy as taking a pencil and
Erasing memories,
But that wouldn't work,
they'd still leave tracks,
Like a deer in the snow.

Coercing me to relive the times you injected me
With tamed kisses.
Like a mother holding her child for the first time.
Creating addictions of desire that would later
sprout from your touch

       My desire is, to not want you this much.

I struggle to reject the dangling fruit that tempts
Taste buds of my emotions
But my flesh is weak, due to the sweetness of potions.
As the high wears down,
My nerves rise like yeast in freshly baked bread
I replay the words you said, "Forever…Goodbye…"
Hoping I could expel them from my head.

Silent tears stop halfway down my face to see if anyone hears
them
F
 A
  L
   L
I can't get rid of you yet.
I climb higher and higher,
Attempting to build the Babel to your heart's desire;
I fail to reach it.

I'm reminded of this shortcoming
Each time I see your face
In pictures, in memories, in dreams…
Recalling the way you used to touch me, like
You were gently lifting broken pieces of glass;
Holding on to me like a poor, broke man
Grasping his last dollar
While the loose change lies low

Me,
Enjoying every moment,
Even the worst,
The rush.

Now,

My heart drifts away from the beating of yours

Like leaves in the

f

a

l

l

Unprepared for

final surrender

I silently wish for a wink of courage, I'm tender

Still,

Leaning as if love would catch me in its arms, but

you're not there

So, I

F

A

L

L

Guess I have to stop leaning

And start standing, just like I used to.

One foot in front of the other,

But this time I don't have to fake this

As I start to refill my half empty cup

with the Absolute vodka of love

I used

to intoxicate you with.

© 2008

The Stage (age 26)

This paper is my canvas,

gray lead is the only color needed to paint this portrait.

Repetitions of lines and curves

riding along music staffs

began to fill the page

As I become alive at last on life's Grand Single stage.

One shot,

one wrong turn,

one right turn,

some get no turn at all

But I

Figure if one of my dreams pass me by

No use in finding dark corners to sit in and cry

There's no one time use in try

Even little trains know how to think they can, so can I.

So yeah,

I'll house old Literature books

found in Thrift stores and Garage sales

teach myself how to become a master of my craft

the one that I say I love so well;

A Subject Matter expert in the topic of literature
Meandering through, the valleys of, talent
Moving hearts like mountains
Imparting certainty in uncertain parts
Instilling hope in hearts
I'm talking, big stuff here;
Dreams don't come with ceilings
That's what makes them dreams.
So I'll give my words engines like rockets and blast baby
Seatbelts are needed because the truth
usually comes with a few bumps in the ride
but you don't sweat as much when you've found your stride

And I'm not missing a beat
No use in wasting your whispering on me
I'm sure you've got dreams of your own
that need to be tended to,
Procrastinations that are begging to be complete
While I'm ova' here beating this pen into submission
Makin it move on missions across this sheet

Because I've made this paper my canvas,

And gray lead is the only color needed to paint this portrait.

Repetitions of lines and curves riding along musical staffs began

to fill the page

And you watch as I,

Become alive on life's

Grand Central stage.

© Summer 2010

In Loving Memory of

Alberta McLemore

Dorothy Robbins

Virginia McLemore

Cheyenne McLemore

'Chick' McLemore

Clarence Robbins

Anita Gray

And

Ms. Ava Moore of *124 Place* for encouraging me,

to *Just Do It* and providing a platform for the Arts,

Poetry and Spoken Word.

Visit the Author Online

www.CleaMcLemore.com

Facebook.com/CleaMcLemore

Twitter.com/theClMac

Instagram.com/theClMac

Pinterest.com/theClMac

author@CleaMcLemore.com

www.ingramcontent.com/pod-product-compliance
Lightning Source LLC
LaVergne TN
LVHW090047090426
835511LV00031B/358